BUILD YOUR BACK THE VINCE GIRONDA WAY

BY GREG SUSHINSKY

Build Your Back the Vince Gironda Way

By Greg Sushinsky

Copyright © 2017 Greg Sushinsky

ISBN-13: 978-1542638142
ISBN-10: 1542638143

Visit Greg's website
Premier Bodybuilding and Fitness
www.premierbodybuildingandfitness.com

NOTE: This book concerns the use of nutritional principles and vigorous exercise programs, which can potentially pose physical risks to anyone who may undertake them. No liability is assumed by the author for the use of any of the information in this book. No medical advice or information is intended or implied. You should always exercise safely and you should first consult your health professionals, physicians and/or nutritionists, before using any of the information contained in this publication.

Table of Contents

Introduction 1

Before You Start 3

Working The Back 4

Vince Anatomy 5

What Not To Do 7

Vince Form 7

Key Techniques For Developing The Back 9

The Vince Gironda Preferred Back Exercises 10

For The Beginner 13

Intermediate Workouts 15

Advanced Workouts 19

Extras: Vince-Style Tips, Techniques, Principles 23

Bonus Workout: Four Exercise Back Workout 25

About Greg Sushinsky 27

Introduction

Working out the Vince Gironda way is both alike and unlike other ways of working out. The exercises sometimes are the same and at other times different than most bodybuilders are used to, but even the techniques for doing them can be unique. So is the case with back work. Developing this large key area for a bodybuilder is part of an ongoing quest for one's own ultimate physique, so the importance and interest in back training is obvious. Vince Gironda's methods offer a promising avenue to back development.

With this in mind we have put together a series of back workouts which bodybuilders can use to progress from whatever stage of current development they're in to continual improvement.

In studying and using many of the Gironda principles for this back training program, we've developed ways of utilizing many of Vince's preferred exercises to construct workouts that are directly in line with his type of training: brief, intense, concentrated. Applying yourself to any of these exercises or routines in the way we've described should benefit just about any bodybuilder. For who has developed to the extent that they can't improve further?

These routines aren't a rehash of Vince's routines, as good as many of those are, but are developed anew in the lineage of his training, largely in conjunction with his ideas. We've also where necessary, as in all our work on Vince Gironda, modified or even embraced challenges to his ideas. Two things: one, where that's done it's to get better results, and two, we do so with great respect for him and his work.

Before You Start

It makes sense to know where you're going before you start on a journey, and it's no different with bodybuilding. After all, you proceed from where you are with the physique development you currently have, to a better place where you've improved your physique. Ideally that's how it should work, and it does if you have a clear plan so you know what to do and how to go about it.

In this case, what you're trying to do is build your back, but you have to keep in mind that you want your back development to blend in with the rest of your physique.

Here's where Vince Gironda's principles already start to shine. To have your back development blend in with the rest of your physique, you have to know Vince's overview of what constituted a good physique; it's what you'll be aiming at.

Vince Gironda favored a physique that featured wide shoulders and a wide back, which tapered to a narrow, slender waist. On the front of the upper body, he advocated building a wide, high chest, balanced arms between biceps, triceps and forearms, with well developed abs, for a complete upper body that had equal development from front to back. The thighs were developed from below the hip to the knee, with prominent calves rounding out the lower body development. No one muscle group or section should overshadow another, and aspects of muscle groups for muscular detail were developed, along with sharp definition. This was sometimes referred to as the "symmetrical" physique, or back in Vince's day, the "Apollo" physique, though more recently it's mostly referred to as the "Classic Physique." The Classic Physique was aspired to by others, more commonly in Vince Gironda's day, most notably the great Steve Reeves.

This style of physique is distinct from the modern-day physique of many bodybuilders, which features all muscle groups developed to maximum size without much regard (or any regard) to proportion or balance. This generally describes the contest winners of today and for the last several decades, particularly in bodybuilding contests which feature massive drug taking. The bodybuilding Vince Gironda advocated and taught was compatible with the ideals of developing an outstanding physique for any natural or drug-free bodybuilder.

Working The Back

Given that the principles of Vince Gironda differ in terms of the type of physique he was trying to build, it follows that Vince's methods might be a little different. And they are. For the standard physique, the style of today where undifferentiated mass is sought after, there's a large emphasis on heavy, basic exercises. Often these are done to the exclusion of other exercises. The champions of today often boast of their massive exercise poundages, less so the massive drug taking that usually gets them there. So back work often features very heavy barbell rows, T-Bar rows, deadlifts with powerlifter poundages, and so on, often done with poor form. What happens when natural, drug-free bodybuilders try this is often problematic. Strength, though often hard to come by, usually greatly outstrips development. Simply put, drug-free bodybuilders often end up with far less impressive back development than they seek. Part of the problem is the exercises, yet much of the problem is the way the exercises are done.

Vince Anatomy

Vince had some definite ideas how your back should develop and look, as we mentioned, according to his principles and in line with his overall vision of a completely developed physique. And you should always keep in mind Vince's overall view of what a superior developed physique should look like, as we've discussed.

Vince Gironda was a self-taught student of anatomy, and felt most bodybuilders were lacking in such critical knowledge. Related to that was kinesiology, or the study of the functioning of the muscles. After all, Vince reasoned, how could you make intelligent choices in selecting exercises and designing workouts if you weren't familiar with the way the muscles worked?

The way Vince Gironda looked at the anatomy of the back was that the most significant areas were the upper and mid-back area. (The lower back or spinal erectors were often considered and worked separately, usually included in leg work.) Vince wanted bodybuilders to concentrate on developing the muscles across the upper back, including the lats but importantly, also, the smaller muscles in the center and the outer regions, such as the infraspinatus and the teres major. The teres major was a particular emphasis for Vince. These are the muscles below the shoulder which add the wide look to the upper back.

Vince of course wanted to develop the lats, but unlike most bodybuilding teachers, wanted to largely avoid lower lat development. He felt excessive lower lat development widened the waist when viewed from behind and spoiled some of the much sought after all-important V-taper.

Although some of his students, most notably Mr. Olympia winner Larry Scott, went after lower lat development to complete the development of their backs, those who were influenced by Vince as Larry Scott was still did it carefully and with an eye toward keeping the waist-widening properties to a minimum.

Other than that, Vince still wanted to get long lat development from the center of the spine, where the lats attach, along with the mid and outer back, with additional back detail as we said, provided by the development of the rhomboids, infraspinatus and teres major and minor. These seemingly small muscles add size, shape and detail to complete a well-developed back.

What Not To Do: Don't Over Develop the Traps

The high traps, with development that dominates even when viewing the physique from the front, is a Vince Gironda no-no. Olympic lifters and powerlifters often feature dominant trap development, or over-development, but the pro bodybuilders in the last couple of decades have taken to developing outsize trapezius muscles, too, which dominate both from the front and back of their physiques. It's a look that spoils symmetry, shape and aesthetics, so Vince Gironda was against it. Therefore, the exercises which develop traps like that, such as heavy power cleans and deadlifts or even shrugs, were not much a part of Vince's world.

What we've discussed is Vince's view of muscle anatomy for the back. Use this to build your back size, yes, but emphasize great shape, detail, definition and aesthetic appeal. Later, we'll see how this anatomy leads into a discussion of the exercises Vince preferred, to obtain this type of back development.

Vince Form

Exercise form was of critical importance for Vince Gironda. In his teachings, the correct use of form – appropriate to whatever the desired outcome was—could often be the difference in meeting your objectives in working out or not. For Vince, exercise performance was more critical than the amount of weight used. He noted that good form on back exercises was sometimes difficult to achieve for trainees, but it was necessary to strive for in building the area correctly to look your best.

Vince most often—but not always, suggested, as he wrote in his First Workout Bulletin, that exercises be done in "good, slow form." This admittedly leaves a lot open to interpretation, yet you can go into any gym or watch even professional bodybuilders work out and know that they're not executing form in that way. Rather than the high-speed, sloppy partial cheating reps with too much weight often employed by bodybuilders, Vince stressed selecting exercise poundages you can handle, then performing the exercise correctly. This meant under control, with tension you could feel, taking at least a couple of seconds on the positive part of the rep, followed by a stop or contraction, then a slow lowering or negative portion of the rep with tension for a couple of seconds under control, with a pause. The whole idea was to work the muscle, not just heave weights around. Performing exercises this way was the best way, Vince felt, to isolate and develop the muscle you were working on.

So strict form was usually the favored method for Vince, and it's especially evident in his suggestion for how to do back exercises. Occasionally, though, he would provide some wrinkles on form, with faster reps and even what he called "creative cheating," a looser though not sloppy rep. The idea was to get at the muscle in a different way, not just fling heavy weights around.

It's important to repeat, though, that the main thing to keep in mind is usually to do the exercises in good slow form, feeling the tension, contraction and extension from beginning to end of the rep, where you pause slightly before starting the next rep. This works the target muscle area thoroughly. After all, you're trying to work the muscle fully to develop it, so Vince Gironda's emphasis on form is an important part of the method to do so.

Key Techniques For Developing The Back

More detail on form and performance

    1. Arch Your Back

    2. Contract & Hold

    3. Non-lockout (Don't Lockout)

These techniques are so important for producing correct form in working the back that Vince emphasized them again and again. Though they are separate techniques, they are related.

1. Arch Your Back: Whether he was recommending pulley work, chinning, or even various special forms of rowing, Vince stressed over and over to arch your back in the performance of the exercise. This usually meant pushing your chest out and drawing your shoulders back. For pulley rowing, this most often stressed the teres major that Vince wanted to work, or to get the correct contraction and feeling in lat work with rows; it was imperative in performing chins the way Vince advised.

What this arching does is better isolate the muscle area you want to work so that the maximum force of the contraction can be applied and tension held during the exercise. It is part of how Vince attempted to wring everything he could out of each exercise.

2. Contract & Hold: Vince often suggested that the trainee contract and hold the weight in the contracted position for a count of one or two seconds. You'll see what a difference this makes when you perform your back exercises, whether it's pulley work, chins or pulldowns. This strong contraction directly engages the muscle fibers you are aiming at and should give you muscle growth and development right where you want it.

3. Non-lockout: To keep the tension and contraction alive throughout the rep, Vince often suggested on the negative part of the rep, say in pulley work, not to let the pulley all the way out. This keeps constant tension on the targeted muscle, makes the exercise more difficult and should yield more muscle growth.

The Vince Gironda Preferred Back Exercises: Pulley Work & Chins

If you have used any of Vince's courses, or read any of his articles for developing the back, or even trained at his gym or under his supervision, you will quickly realize that Vince often favored different exercises than the standard ones to develop the back. Most of the exercises Vince used throughout his courses and training of others were centered around two kinds of movements: pulley movements and chins.

Vince used a variety of pulley movements as he felt they targeted specific muscles or even specific areas of the muscles. He also utilized chins in back workouts in different ways—and often in different ways than their standard exercise performance, again, to get at the back muscles more effectively. Think of the standard use only of say, rows and perhaps deadlifts as being more general movements, whereas Gironda considered the exercises he chose to use as isolation exercises. Some analysis will show that this isn't strictly true, but on a relative basis it certainly is. Pulley rows, for example, can be used to isolate muscle areas of the back better than heavy rows.

As with many of Vince's ideas, you should be able to get what he was driving at even if Vince might not have expressed it exactly right. For example, how can you do a set of heaving, cheating, heavy barbell rows and target the exercise toward the teres major, or at least the wide, high area of the back that runs just under the shoulder blades? Or even the mid-back area or even lats for mass? Hard to do when you're trying to lift more weight than you should, with an exercise that's much more general than specific.

And although Vince believed in using appropriate exercise poundages, meaning heavy when it was called for, the tendency to use far too much weight in sloppy form on the standard exercises is a peril for bodybuilders Gironda was trying to avoid. Rowing has its place, for example—various forms were occasionally deployed by Vince, but cheat rows with too much weight don't develop the back properly and are an invitation to injury.

A third type of exercise was included in the Gironda back work prescriptions: hyperextensions for the lower back. Vince preferred this to deadlifts (even stiff-leg deadlifts), power cleans and the like, as hypers were easier on the spine yet yielded that cord-like development of the erectors, without either the massive depletion of energy from deadlifts, along with their potential hip-widening effects and their likely chance of injuring non-super human bodybuilders. As we mentioned, Vince often included lower back work with leg workouts instead, so that's where he usually included hyperextensions. But for the rest of the back, Vince emphasized pulley work, chins and related moves, for the most part. Now let's look at a routine.

For The Beginner

The trainee just starting out bodybuilding needs to do a workload he or she can manage, while building the most important aspects of the physique to start out right. Vince Gironda most often recommended one exercise per bodypart, where a bodybuilder would develop the most important area of a muscle group, then move on to other undeveloped areas. Beginners especially were encouraged to follow this path, though he often recommended this for advanced bodybuilders, too. Don't, however, let the designation of beginner, intermediate and advanced levels become absolutes. They are meant as important guidelines.

In his classic "First Workout Bulletin," Vince recommended bodybuilders begin with one exercise per muscle group for three sets of eight reps (3 x 8), while working the whole body three times a week. In that routine, Vince recommended Lat Pulls for his standard beginner back routine.

Although in his written courses Vince usually favored Lat Pulls, (also sometimes designated as Long Pulley Rows or Long Pulls by him), which develop largely the mid back, remember the earlier material where we pointed out that Vince also believed in chinning work. The problem with chins, especially the way Vince sometimes suggested doing them, is that they were often beyond the strength or ability of novice bodybuilders. To get a similar effect with a more workable exercise, we'll suggest for our Vince-style beginner workout, overhead lat pulldowns on a lat machine instead.

So here's the beginner back workout:

I. Overhead Pulldowns 3 x 8

These pulldowns should be done to the front, with a shoulder width or slightly wider than shoulder width grip. Choose a poundage slightly less than you think you can handle in strict form for your first workouts. You can add weight later. Anchor yourself either seated or kneeling in front of the lat machine, then pull steadily and evenly down to the chest, pause, then control the return movement. Remember to arch your back, contract the back at the pause, and keep good form throughout.

Overhead pulldowns will work the length of the lat, a large area, if done correctly, much in the way that a properly done chin would. This exercise allows the beginner to use some weight resistance while the tracking of the machine makes keeping good form easier than chins or even lat pulls.

A second, or alternate beginner's workout for the back would utilize medium grip chins.

So, the second beginner workout is simply this:

II. Medium Grip Chins 3 x 8

Medium grip chins should be done to the front, where you pull yourself up in a smooth, steady motion, without swinging your legs or arms. You should try to chin yourself as high as the mid-pec level, or at least the top of your chest. If you have trouble doing the reps, as it takes some strength, you can do what Vince called "singles," where you disengage the arms each rep. Chins of any kind can be difficult for new bodybuilders lacking strength, so if this is too hard, you may want to stick with the overhead pulldown workout until you can do chins.

These medium grip chins will also work the length of the lat. Remember to use the same good form, arching your back and contracting, then controlling the lowering of your body from the bar. This exercise, because of its difficulty, can provide a transition into intermediate workouts for bodybuilders who can't do it effectively as beginners but are better able to handle it as they progress.

Don't let the stark simplicity of these two beginner routines make you think that you need more. When you work these exercises hard and successfully do this workout you'll make progress, develop more muscle and get used to the workload, then you can eventually add some sets. But be careful; don't do too much work because if you work the whole body routine hard, you can overtrain on it.

Intermediate Workouts

(Note: First intermediate workout can be Chins, 4 x 8, from preceding group, as we discussed.)

III. Long Lat Pulls 4 x 8 to 6 x 6

Although Vince Gironda often included this exercise in beginners' workouts, we feel it's a little better suited to intermediates, someone who's been training for awhile and has developed some muscle. The style of performance of this exercise is critical. You should lean forward with your knees slightly bent, your feet against a board or stops. Then you pull the handle back so your chest is at a 90 degree angle to the floor, with your back arched and the muscles contracted. Then reverse the movement under control. Always keep the movement smooth. This exercise works the upper and middle lats, and is really an important one for overall back development.

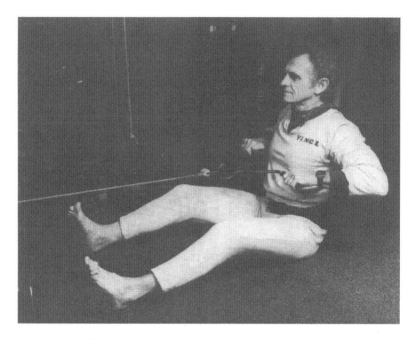

A couple of notes. Some would say the 4 sets of 8 is not part of Vince's scheme; while Vince didn't commonly recommend it, he occasionally did. Besides, we are creating with and extending Vince's methods, especially when this works in a "Vince-ish" way. Intermediates can also work up to six sets of six reps (6 x 6) on this with good results.

Vince sometimes called long lat pulls by various names: lat pulls, long pulls, horizontal pulls, long floor pulls—but it's the long pulley row or seated cable row. It's all the same exercise.

Vince felt this exercise was so important he included it in many back workouts, including his famous definition course and many other advanced workouts. We feel it's especially well suited for intermediate and advanced bodybuilders.

If you don't have access to pulleys, you can carefully substitute barbell or dumbbell rows, but be sure to emphasize form as we described, and use more moderate weights, feeling the movement.

The next workout will focus on developing the teres major, an emphasis that can add a high, wide dimension to the back, as well as detail across the upper ridge.

IV. Short Pulley Row 4 x 8

This exercise is similar to the long pulley row but is a different movement, as the pulley set up should allow for pulling at an angle that really hits the teres major. You pull to the mid-chest line and contract the teres. If you've already done the long pulley, you should be able to get the hang of this fairly easily.

If your gym lacks the set up for the short pulley row, you can substitute overhead leaning pulldowns. Lean forward at the start then as you pull down to the front, lean back. Reverse the movement as you allow the bar to rise and return to the start position.

The next workout features two exercises. By the time you're an intermediate, you will likely be working on a split routine of four or five total days per week. You may be working your back two or three times along with other muscle groups.

Exercise Combinations

This is an important concept in the Vince Gironda way of training. While Vince often recommended one exercise per bodypart at a time, then moving on to another exercise weeks or months later to develop another aspect of the muscle group, he did use exercise combinations. Unlike many of the workouts you'll see where bodybuilders simply throw together exercises for various muscle groups, Vince often had precise ideas of what areas to work and which ones not to work. More than that, he tried to choose exercises that would go together so that the sum of effectiveness and development would be greater than the individual parts. You can see our attempt to follow his lead in the two intermediate workouts which follow.

The next intermediate workout features two exercises:

V. 1. Long Lat Pulls 3 x 8

2. Short Pulley Row 3 x 8

This workout emphasizes the development of the upper and middle back, actually the belly of the lat for mass and thickness with the long lat pulls (or seated cable rows or other various names we discussed) and the width and detail under the shoulders with the short pulley row and the teres major development. The smaller but no less important muscles along the upper back such as the infraspinatus and rhomboids are also developed via the short pulley row.

This combination of two kinds of pulls for the back can result in significant gains in both thickness and detail.

VI. Wide Grip Chins (to Front) 3 x 8

Long Lat Pulls 3 x 8

This is another intermediate workout which can boost your back development significantly. The chins, this time with a wider grip, though still performed to the front (i.e., pull up to your chest), will strongly work the center of your lats. The long pulls will again develop the mass and thickness in the middle part of your back, often a neglected area among bodybuilders.

Advanced Workouts

When bodybuilders have progressed in overall development, including shape, definition, detail and muscle size, and have learned how successfully to work through many different types of workouts and exercises, they might be ready for more advanced work. This is usually an individual matter, though. Everyone should proceed at their own pace. Some will continue to reap benefits from what we've termed beginner workouts all through their bodybuilding days. So again, don't get hung up on the category of these workouts, whether they're termed beginning, intermediate or advanced.

That said, when you feel ready to tackle more advanced workouts, it helps to have the confidence from having success on the previous workouts that led up to them. Makes sense. The real value in grouping these exercises from the simpler, somewhat easier to the more complex and more difficult is that a bodybuilder can target what he or she needs then choose the right workout to go after it.

So for advanced bodybuilders, there will be the opportunity to do more volume work, or greater intensity and to use various intensity techniques.

The first advanced workout looks familiar:

VII. Long Lat Pulls 8 x 8

This is part of a one-exercise per muscle group workout that usually splits the body three ways, spread out over six days per week. The one back exercise featured will be the familiar Long Lat Pulls (i.e., Seated Cable Rows, etc.), which have been featured prominently in the intermediate workouts. But the element of doing eight sets is what raises the challenge to an advanced level. This will again be an emphasis on the mid-back area and develop muscle thickness.

Vince Gironda included this exercise in his beginners' workouts, as we said, and also in his advanced definition course, and included it along with other workouts in some of his advanced courses. Here we're including it in an advanced course where a bodybuilder is specializing more on mass.

You should rest only a minute or less between sets, though, and Vince often challenged trainees to diminish the rest periods over time, which was an intensity technique.

Our next advanced workout follows a similar pattern as the Long Lat Pulls.

VIII. Medium Grip Chins (to Front) 8 x 8

Again, this exercise was the basis of earlier workouts, but now the volume has been ramped up so the bodybuilder can thoroughly saturate the length of the lats for potentially greater gains in lat width. Many bodybuilders have a hard time chinning, so this workout, even though it doesn't look like much on paper, can be tough.

IX. Short Pulley Row 8 x 8

You can really blast the teres major and upper back to build ridges of muscle with eight sets of these. It's an area that Vince Gironda felt was lacking in many bodybuilders so he emphasized this all the way through in his instruction. For many advanced bodybuilders, this, along with lower back work (hyperextensions) can put the finishing touches on an otherwise impressively developed back.

Compound Sets:

The next advanced workout features compound movements. These are two exercises for different aspects of the same muscle group performed one after another in succession, nonstop.

X. Medium Grip Chins 3 x 6 + Short Pulley Rows 3 x 6 (Compounds)

(Total of 6 sets of 6 reps or 3 compound sets of 12 for the two exercises together)

Medium grip chins should be done to the front. Pull high to the chest. Do 6 reps, then immediately follow these with short pulley rows, also for 6 reps. That's one compound set. The medium grip chins work the length of the lat while the short pulley rows concentrate on the teres, for that important upper back development.

Doing each set of exercise without resting in between adds intensity and difficulty, but there is less chance of overworking the muscles since you are targeting different aspects of the back, as well as keeping the sets to only a few. Depending on how you count these, as six individual sets or 3 compound sets, in spite of the relatively low set volume, this is a very intense and productive workout. Accomplished individuals with tremendous energy can eventually work up to 4 sets of 6 reps on each exercise (the equivalent of 8 sets if counted separately, a total of 4 compound sets of 12 total reps for the two exercises together).

XI. Long Lat Pulls, 3 x 6 + Medium Grip Chins 3 x 6 (Compounds)

(Total of 6 sets of 6 reps or 3 compound sets of 12 reps for the two exercises together.)

The long lat pulls will work a great deal of lat area, notably the upper and middle part, while the chins will work the length of the lats. There will be some overlap here, as this is a highly concentrated lat workout, intensified by the compound sets. Still, it's a worthwhile back-blasting workout for an advanced bodybuilder which should deliver both mass and width. Most, even accomplished advanced bodybuilders, will find this routine surprisingly challenging and extremely effective. Again, if you are up to it, eventually you can work up to that fourth set of compounds, which is the equivalent or 8 total sets of 6 reps each or 4 sets of 12 compounds. Either way you count it, it's an effective workout

XII. Long Lat Pulls 4 x 12

For another advanced workout, we return to the one-exercise per bodypart theme so dear to Vince Gironda, and employ the long lat pull for overall lat development. The difference here is that the rep scheme is higher, although the sets are similar to some of the previous workouts, both advanced and intermediate. This workout, however, with the strict form and the high tempo can be very demanding. You are doing 50% more reps while striving to keep good form with whatever is a challenging exercise poundage for you. You may have to fight hard to complete all the reps in good form. Done with intense effort, this workout can ramp up your work load to build more lat muscle than you thought possible.

Extras: Vince-Style Tips, Advanced Techniques, Principles

Concentration: In addition to using the kind of form Vince recommends (covered earlier), he always insisted that the bodybuilder strive to train with strict concentration, and to attack each workout. This energy helps provide the necessary intensity for muscle growth. Vince believed in this for working all muscle groups, and it's certainly necessary with such a large and important area as the back.

Intensity: There are many ways to use intensity. In addition to concentration and strict form, Vince was a big advocate for limiting rest time between sets. The goal was for a fast, high-tempo workout, with reps done in good form with challenging poundages, yet not training to failure, which he considered a form of overtraining. The Vince Gironda type of intense workout was a goal to shoot for, to keep working at. With these back workouts, you can accomplish a lot of work in a short period of time.

Burns: These are short, partial reps, as little as 1to 2 inches done at the end of a full rep. In the advanced courses where a bodybuilder might be doing 4 sets of 8 reps, on the last rep of one or eventually all four sets he might utilize burns. These can be very taxing but can provide extra growth. Larry Scott was famously a big user of this technique.

Hyperextensions: This exercise, as we mentioned, develops your lower back and erectors. Just a reminder to include these at times in your leg workout, as Vince preferred, if you are not doing them along with your back exercises.

Hard Gainers: Vince recommended to keep workouts brief, one exercise per bodypart, usually no more than 3-4 sets of 6-8 reps, work each muscle group twice per week. The beginner exercises for back work are excellent for this. If you want to choose alternate exercises, remember to keep the sets and reps down.

Specialization: If you want to add volume to specialize on your back, then cut the rest of your workout down. For example, if you are doing 6 x 6 on all your muscle groups, featuring one exercise each, but decide to do three back exercises for 3 x 8 each (total of 9 sets of back work), cut back on your other muscle groups to 3 or 4 sets.

Another way to specialize is to intensify your workout. The example of adding burns or other intensity techniques, such as one-and-a-half reps can promote muscle gains without adding volume.

Stretch & Pose: Vince was an advocate of practicing posing, but you can take this advice to another level. When you pose the back you often flex the lats. This can help stretch the area. Add to this hanging from a chinning bar and other shoulder and back stretches which at least can help you enhance the appearance of your back width, if not actually widen the area.

Bonus Workout: Four Exercise Back Workout

This is a really effective workout work out for an advanced bodybuilder, four exercises done one set each with 30 seconds to 1 minute rest between sets. Vince even advocated doing this type of workout for a total of 4 sets of 12 reps with no rest between exercises. This may be too much for most bodybuilders, so begin with 4 x 8 and work up to the 4 x 12 nonstop if you can. It's a workout that promotes lots of growth, detail and overall great back gains. Here it is.

Four-Way Back Workout

    1. Long Pulley Rows

    2. Medium Grip Chins (to front)

    3. Short Pulley Rows

    4. Overhead Pulldowns

Modifications: Individualize. Vince maintained that most successful bodybuilders were specializing much of the time. By this he meant they didn't perform cookie-cutter workouts, but were constantly adjusting and adapting to changes in their physique and exercise results. If you find exercises that work for you, even in combinations that Vince Gironda might not have approved, use them. The same with sets and reps and even exercise performance.

Eventually construct your own workouts based on what you learn. Vince often suggested to simplify and cut back if you aren't getting results, a key bit of advice.

As we've written in all our work on Vince Gironda, whether it's exercise or diet, you have to pursue that which works for you. Use the best ideas, principles and techniques of Vince and go from there. Work out, analyze your results, learn, and chart your individualized journey.

We hope with the workouts and ideas we've given you here that you will build the best back you possibly can. We wish you great training!

About Greg Sushinsky

Greg Sushinsky is a natural bodybuilder who has trained for several years. He is a professional writer who has written extensively about bodybuilding, with numerous training articles appearing in MuscleMag International, Ironman magazine, Reps! and others. He continues to train hard and enthusiastically. He strives to maintain a lean, proportionate physique, writes and publishes on bodybuilding, and continues to do and pursue many writing and publishing projects in his other areas of interest. He continues to advise and consult with bodybuilders, athletes and fitness people.

Books by Greg Sushinsky

Training and Eating the Vince Gironda Way

Training and Eating the Steve Reeves Way

The Hard Gainer Report

The Natural Bodybuilding Training Manual

Visit Greg's website
Premier Bodybuilding and Fitness
www.premierbodybuildingandfitness.com

Manufactured by Amazon.ca
Bolton, ON